SUPERSIZE YOUR STORY-TELLING SKILLS

Britt Malka

What's the Point?

I woke up one morning at 5 am and got the idea for this book.

I thought, "Wouldn't it be cool to have a new story writing drill for each month in the year? It could be a challenge."

The more I thought about it, the more I liked the idea.

I had already made a couple of courses that included drills, so I knew how effective they can be.

Why Drills?

There's a reason why the army does drills.

No sergeant has ever told his troops to go read a book or watch a movie about how to get fit.

No. They make their soldiers do drills. They practice the same thing, day in and day out, until they can do what they need to do without even thinking.

It's become ingrained.

It works with writing, too.

Look at the following sentence, for example:

"Angela was sad because her pet rat had just died."

It makes you go, "Yeah, right," right?

Then look at the following two examples of saying the same thing, but differently:

Example one: "The teardrops welled up in Angela's eyes, onto her eyelashes then rolled down her cheeks and dripped onto the cloth cubbyhole Freddy slept in. Item by item she removed his toys, the water bowl and his spinning wheel. Her tears flowed - one by one, drop by drop."

Example two: "Biggy was the rat that had survived, until today. Her and Biggy. Angela lifted the framed selfie, brushed off the few flecks of dust she had missed, and replaced it on the long, narrow table alongside the others: Biggy, Tiny, Biggy and Tiny, her and Tiny, the three of them. Angela sank into the chair facing the photos and cried."

The two examples are written by students of my *Show, Don't Tell Drills* course. In it, we start small and add more and more layers. Until you get results like the above examples.

Drills work so well because you train your muscles until the movements become automatic.

Even writing muscles work that way.

You can use drills to train yourself to get better at writing stories, too.

Where Can You Use Stories?

Stories are useful in many situations.

If you're writing fiction, obviously.

But also if you're writing nonfiction.

Stories in nonfiction make the text more memorable and more entertaining.

Stories create images and movies in our heads.

For example, my husband has always gotten stung by mosquitoes.

While we sit in the same room, the small stinging beasts fly in his direction and suck his blood.

That means that shortly after he'll be scratching several red spots on his arms and legs.

We had a few candles that were meant to repel the bloodsuckers, but once we ran out of them, my husband needed something else. So we went to a pharmacy.

How do you say "mosquito" in Hebrew?

I had no idea. Neither had my husband. We looked for something on the shelves but found nothing. So my husband stopped one of the pharmacists and did this:

"Ani rotzeh…" (I want – so far so good)

"Bzzzzzz…" he said and moved his hand around in the air like a flying mosquito. He jerked his fingers down on his arm, and then he made scratching movements.

The pharmacist bent over with laughter and gave him a bottle with some balm that should repel the flying terrorists.

She understood.

And my husband had used only body language to get his message through.

When we look back in time – way, way back to some of the first human beings on Earth – they probably didn't have a language at first. They must have used sounds and body language to communicate.

What they left for us, carved in stone or painted on walls, were images. And their images formed stories.

Some of the first alphabets were images – like the Egyptian and the Aramaic drawings.

We understand images well. And you can build images by telling stories.

Easier to Understand

Stories are for anything. They work for any kind of writing or speaking.

One of the reasons is that it's easier to understand a story than grasping mere facts. Let me illustrate this with an example.

Do this test:

Take a look at what Wiki has to tell you about Touraine: http://en.wikipedia.org/wiki/Touraine

It's a short text, so don't worry.

Have you read it?

Good.

Now close your eyes and tell me about Touraine.

You might remember a few things, but I bet that it wouldn't be that much.

Let's try this instead…

When my husband, the kids and I decided to move to

France in 1999, we disagreed about where to live.

I was born in Denmark - a cold (freezing cold) country, so I wanted to go to Southern France, to the sun and the sea.

My husband preferred colder areas, so he talked about going to Northern France.

We asked some French friends we knew through the Internet their opinion, and one of them, Michael, said to us:

"You should go to Touraine. It's in the middle of France, and it will take you two hours to go to the sea. It's only two hours away from Paris, and if you want mountains… well, they are only two hours away, too."

So we went to Tours, the "capital" of Touraine, to see if we could find a place there to live. The waiter in the hotel where we were staying, said to us:

"There are several beautiful towns in Touraine, but the prettiest and most charming is Amboise."

We went for a drive, and after a turn in the road, we were suddenly presented with a view over the river and a castle. That view was stunning. Then we saw the city sign: Amboise.

We lived there for a couple of years, and it was a fantastic city.

We often visited old castles, of which there were plenty in Touraine. We even spent a weekend in a castle, once. That was pure luxury and very relaxing.

…

How much more would you be able to tell me about

Touraine now?

That's the power of storytelling.

It's fun to write, and it creates images in the head of the reader. Even though it's non-fiction.

It's easier to remember.

Because a story leaves an image in the head of the reader (or listener) it makes stuff easier to remember. So if you want to help your readers remember what you wrote, then you should add stories.

It's entertaining.

Even dull topics can be entertaining if you include stories.

Stories Sell, Too

A story—on its own—can sell for you. That's why stories work so well on sales pages and in emails.

There are numerous examples of this.

After the movie *Top Gun* came out, the Ray-Ban sales went up 40%, and more young people joined the army.

After *101 Dalmatians*, more people than usual chose that breed for their next dog.

Neither of these movies told people to go out and buy stuff. They just told a story. The story did the selling.

You May Not Be Familiar with Writing Stories

That's okay. We'll be doing lots of drills here, so you'll get it. Even if you start from scratch.

This is how we'll do this.

Every day, for six or seven days a week, you will sit down for five minutes and write.

I recommend you do this in the morning, because otherwise there's a risk that you'll postpone it until later. And later has the bad habit of never happening.

So every morning (best), you open this book, pick the present month, and do the drill for five minutes.

Unless I give instructions to write something in longhand, you can choose whether you want to write on your computer, on your phone/tablet, or in a notebook.

To get into the good habit of doing your daily drills, I recommend that you download and print out a calendar. You can do so for free at https://print-a-calendar.com.

Then every time you've done your daily drills, mark that day with a big cross, and see them string together like a necklace.

How do you track your five minutes? You can use an alarm on your phone, a timer, or an online stopwatch that you can find here: https://www.online-stopwatch.com/countdown-timer/

Five Senses

Whenever possible, use all five senses in your writing.

You want your reader to feel that they are physically experiencing your story, and an easy way to obtain that is by involving as many senses as possible.

The five senses are:

Sight
Sound
Smell
Taste
Touch

At first, if you're not used to writing about the five senses, you will find it difficult.

To make it easier, I recommend that you use one sense per day.

If the drill exercise told you to describe a square of dark chocolate, the first day or two, you could describe it by focusing on sight.

Describe the dark-brown, almost black color. Describe the shape of the piece of chocolate.

Then, when you're familiar with describing the sight, switch to sound.

Does the piece of chocolate make any sounds? Not likely, but a person who eats it may make sounds. Or if you drop it on the floor, it makes a sound. Or your dog may sit and stare at the chocolate, making clucking sounds with its tongue. (Don't give chocolate to dogs, by the way. It's poisonous for them.)

When this feels comfortable for you, use both sight and sound in your daily drill.

Then add smell. Then taste. Then touch.

If the object has no taste of its own, the smell can

sometimes provoke a certain taste in your mouth. That works fine.

At other times, you may need to leave out taste if nothing relates to it at all in your story-drill.

Touch can be difficult, in my experience.

Think of touch in more than one way.

You can palpate something with your fingers to explore a surface. But your whole body can also "touch" something and feel the temperature.

If we go back to the piece of chocolate, then a morning drill could look like this:

Next to me on my desk, there's a piece of dark chocolate. I'm not a super-fan of chocolate, but since I haven't had any breakfast yet, the dark brown square keeps grabbing my attention. It's so smooth on the surface that it's almost inviting me to just touch it with my tongue, and bite my teeth into it, leaving a mark that would be smaller than the name of the chocolate company, which is marked on the top of the chocolate, back when it was still hot and fluid.

The dark, almost black color tells me that this piece of chocolate will taste both bitter and sweet. Bitter, because of the 90% cocoa it contains, and sweet because of the added sugar that is not good for my health.

As the temperature in the room …

And this was how far I got in five minutes. I was about to write about how the temperature released scents of chocolate into the air.

During the five minutes I wrote, I described the sight of the chocolate, some touch, and the taste.

If I had had more time, I would have continued with smell and sound like this:

As the temperature in the room interacts with the chocolate, scents of cocoa drift into my nostrils and make my stomach growl.

My dog, Nefnef, sits next to me. Her nose points toward my desktop, and from time to time she smacks her lips and licks her muzzle.

That would have covered all five senses.

Will That Not Be Boring After a While?

Yes, and that's on purpose.

If you were to describe a piece of chocolate, sitting next to you, every day for a month, chances are that it will be like this:

The first days: You focus on describing the chocolate, using one sense per day.

Later: You go for the challenge and add more senses.

Later again: Wow, all five senses are involved.

Later again: Oh, gosh, now that you know how to do it, where's the challenge? Hey, wait! This piece of chocolate could be something else. How about an alien lifeform?

That's it. Go normal first, add as many senses as you can, then, as boredom follows, allow your imagination to run wild. Go crazy.

Story Structure

If the whole point is that these drills should make you better at writing stories, then it makes sense to introduce you to story structure.

If you're a novelist, you probably know all about The Hero's Journey, Save the Cat! and other structures.

That's great. I won't repeat them here.

But when you write emails, sales pages, or blog posts, we need a shorter structure.

And the shortest of them all is this one:

A story consists of a *beginning*, a *middle*, and an *end*.

Traditionally, the beginning reflects the present situation. How things are now.

In the middle, all the cool stuff happens. Lots of conflict and tension. Things, maybe even life and death, are at stake. The hero must conquer his enemies in a big fight.

And then we reach the end, which is—hopefully—a happy ending.

Both your beginning and your end are short and make up half of your story together. The middle makes up the rest of the story.

Can You Use Story Structure During These Drills?

Perhaps not at first. But keep the structure in mind, and sooner or later it will come through in your writing.

You grew up listening to stories. Stories are ingrained in our brains, and the structure has been the same for thousands of years.

You already know the structure of stories without thinking about it. Now you'll learn to come out with tiny stories in five minutes. And you'll get better at describing ordinary things in ways that will make others love reading about them.

Isn't This a Waste of Time?

Writing is never a waste of time. Every time you write, you have the chance of getting better.

Besides, you can perhaps use those short exercises.

Do you write emails to a list?

Well, now you have on average 30 ways per month to start your emails with a story.

If you don't have a mailing list, you can use them when you write to friends or family.

Instead of just telling your aunt Amanda from Alaska how the weather is right now in California, you can use one of your January drills to show her how the weather is.

Have fun with those drills, whether or not you choose to use them for other purposes as well.

This Is Not Important

When you write something you think is important, your writing can so easily become stifled and boring.

That's why these drills are not important. They are for your eyes only.

Share them if you like, but know that you don't have to.

These are just drills, nothing important.

Think of it like doing push-ups.

If you had the television recording your every tiny move—the way you put down your fingers on the ground, the way your t-shirt is placed, its color, its shape etc., you would become nervous. If a camera were to zoom in on your arms, and you knew that millions of people would be watching... Wouldn't you be scared?

I would. And I would probably tell the cameraman to come back another day when I was more prepared.

And then I would move to a new address and keep it secret.

If, on the other hand, I was alone in a room, getting down on the floor and doing one push-up, I could do it. (Well, maybe not, but it wouldn't be embarrassing, because nobody would know about it.)

That's how you should see these drills.

They are yours.

And Yet, It's Important

It's important to do the drills every day, six or seven

days a week. Because your story-writing skills will get better and better.

If you skip a day, just get back to them the next day. Aim at never skipping two days in a row.

One day, then get back.

No days, even better.

Five minutes, every day.

You can do it.

You Can Do It

Here's how to proceed:

1. Go to this month's chapter.
2. Read about the drill of the month.
3. Open a text editor or a notebook.
4. Set the timer to five minutes.
5. Write. Stop after five minutes, even in the middle of a sentence.

January

Your January drill is:

What is the weather like?

For five minutes daily, you must write about the weather. Describe how it is, how it feels, how it makes you feel, why it makes you feel that way, what it reminds you of, how it smells, how it tastes, and how it sounds.

If you haven't been outside yet and don't know how the weather is, then use the previous day's weather.

When you do this for a month, your skills will improve, because you'll get tired of writing the same old stuff.

Maybe you'll even come up with parts of stories.

Some tips:

Don't just write: It's 77 degrees outside (25 degrees Celsius). Show the temperature. Does it make you sweat? Do you feel like going to the beach to lie down in the sand, allowing the sun to warm your skin?

Don't write: today it is freezing cold either. Show it. Do you wrap your coat around you to protect your body parts from freezing off? Have you found your old mittens, but even while wearing them, do your fingers go numb so you can't even bend them. Do tiny icicles form in your nostrils?

If you saw yourself from the outside through another person's eyes, what would you see? That's how you can show the temperature or whether it's raining or the sun is shining.

Allow your imagination to run amok. It's raining, sure. Now hyperbole it with a story. For example, check your bank account to see if you have enough money to buy a little boat to get you over the lake that has appeared overnight outside your house.

Or become something else. Swim through the streets as a dolphin. Or a mermaid.

Start with the ordinary at the beginning of January. Then go crazier and crazier during the month. Add more story.

January's Drill

1. Check how the weather is.
2. Write about it for five minutes.

February

Your February drill is:
Wash your hands.
And describe it.

Remember, you have five minutes, so it's not enough to write: I washed my hands.

You need to fill all **five minutes**, and you need to use all **five senses** if possible.

How warm was the water? (Don't tell...show the temperature.) How did you move your hands? How did the soap feel? How did it smell? Hopefully, you didn't taste the soap, but did the smell somehow make your mouth taste the soap anyway? Or did you take a sip of water afterwards, and you can describe its taste?

Here's a reminder of what the five senses consist of:
Sight
Sound
Smell
Taste
Touch

When I write, I have those five senses in a document note next to my writing space in Scrivener.

If you write in other editors, you can have a little post-it note or sticky note next to you where you've written down the five senses.

Every time you use one of the senses in your writing, cross it off.

When you start to get bored writing about how the water made your knuckles hurt until your hands had warmed up, and how you moved your hands around, then it's time to start using your imagination.

Why are you washing your hands?

Is it symbolic? Are you about to perform a big operation and your happiness depends on whether or not your patient survives? Or did you just fall outside, landing in a puddle of mud, and now the raw smell of earth mingles with the lavender soap, while you scrub your hands with a brush under the flowing water?

Let boredom drive you into brilliant descriptions.

Have fun with this drill. And in case you hate it, then look at the bright side of things: February is the shortest month of the year. You only have to do this 28 or 29 times.

February's Drill
1. Wash your hands.
2. Describe it.

March

Your March drill is:

Drink water.

You decide what kind of water you want to drink.

I start my day with a cup of hot water and freshly squeezed lemon juice.

After that, I drink sparkling water with nothing added. No sugar, no juice, nothing.

The temperature of the water varies throughout my day.

In the morning, it's hot. I have to blow air over my cup before I take the first sip.

Later, it's cold, coming directly from the refrigerator. We have a bottle standing nearby all the time, so as time passes, the water becomes lukewarm.

This all affects my impression of the water and how it affects me.

How about you?

Write for five minutes every day in March about how you experience the water you just drank.

Use all five senses:

Sight

Sound
Smell
Taste
Touch

What does your water look like? Hopefully, it's clear and not anything like the brown, muddy water Marty McFly drinks in *Back to the Future 3*.

What does it sound like? If your water is silent, then it's probably not sparkling water. But try whirling it around in the glass.

What does it smell like? Taste like? How does it feel when you touch the glass, or the water is in your mouth? Cold? Hot?

And once you get bored of writing about the mundane, let your imagination run wild.

Become the water and experience how it feels to be in a glass.

Or become a tiny creature that lives in the water.

No idea is too crazy. Just have fun with it and create small stories around everyday things.

March's Drill
1. Drink water.
2. Describe it.

April

Your April drill is:

Pick one event that happened the previous day.

"Nothing happened," you may say. But that's not true.

Something probably happened every minute you were awake, and even while sleeping, things happen. (They are often called "dreams.")

An event doesn't need to be unusual. It can be anything normal.

You walk your dog, and you see a cat.

You feed your fish, and it comes to pick up its food.

Your spouse made dinner.

You drank coffee in the morning.

You read a chapter of a new book on the balcony in your bathrobe.

If you're not doing this drill first thing in the morning, feel free to pick any event that happened today.

Otherwise, just pick an event. Don't linger on this task. Spend one minute, max, picking one.

This drill will have an immense impact on your story-telling skills. It will teach you how any event can be used.

Famous and funny scriptwriter Ricky Gervais said that he got bad grades at school when writing essays. His teacher told him to "write about what you know," but little Ricky didn't listen.

Until one day, when he was desperate enough he did it. And that changed his life forever.

On a personal and much smaller note, I once wrote an essay about using a defective curling iron, and it gave me a top grade.

Should you run out of events, then don't shy away from inventing some along the way.

Maybe you ran into your neighbor who had forgotten to put on his human-mask, and you discovered that he was an alien.

Maybe a creature cried for help in your bathroom, and you found a mermaid in there.

Maybe you stepped in a giant pile of dung and looked up to see an over-sized unicorn.

Or maybe a more ordinary event like you just received the Nobel peace prize.

I'll leave it up to you.

April's Drill

1. Pick an event that happened yesterday.
2. Describe it.

May

Your May drill is:

Hand copy story beginnings.

"What??" I hear you yell.

"Hand copy as in copy...by hand?"

Yes, actually. This month's drill is all about using your hand to write and not your computer. I'll tell you why in a moment.

First, the full assignment.

Go to your bookshelf and find four books you really like. You're going to use one book per week.

If you don't have any books, then go to Amazon and find four best-sellers. You can use the "Look inside" feature for your drills.

Four books, four weeks... That means that you may have two days without any books. Feel free to spend the first of those two days picking the books. And feel free to choose whichever book you liked the most for the last one.

Then each day, start with chapter one and hand copy as much as you can in five minutes.

Why?

This is a piece of advice I've heard many times, mostly from copywriters.

It all started (as far as I know) with Gary Halbert, one of the biggest copywriters ever. (And if you're not into copywriting, you may wonder what it is. It's writing content that sells. It can be sales pages, ads, emails...)

When Gary Halbert taught his son, Bond, to become a copywriter, he didn't give him a course. He told him to copy proven ads by hand.

Why does this work? AWAI (American Writers & Artists Institute) wrote a blog post about it, in which they explain:

"It's been proven time and again that hand writing something you want to learn is effective because you stimulate a part of your brain called the Reticular Activating System (RAS). According to LifeHacker, "The RAS acts as a filter for everything your brain needs to process, giving more importance to the stuff that you're actively focusing on at that moment — something that the physical act of writing brings to the forefront.

"And a study from Human Brain Mapping proved that when you read AND copy something by hand, you also activate the left rolandic operculum, which is associated with sentence-level syntactic encoding. Basically, in laymen's terms, this means when you simply read something, your brain is focused on figuring out the meaning of what you're reading. But, when you write out what you're reading, your brain is more engaged and is focused on the syntax as well as the meaning."

As I said, I had heard this method has been used by copywriters for a long time. A year or so ago, I learned that this tip could also be used by fiction writers. I learned this in a workshop by Dean Wesley Smith, who is one of the most prolific writers of all time.

In other words: whether you want to convince people to do something with your writing or you want to become a better fiction writer, this is a drill that will get you far.

May's Drill

1. Find four books.

2. Pick one book each week and hand copy the beginning.

June

Your June drill is:

Describe yesterday's dinner.

Do you even remember what you had for dinner last night?

Honestly, I don't always.

It's such an ingrained part of everyday life that we forget about it.

But all everyday events can be turned into great little stories. Stories you can use in emails, in books, or even on sales pages.

This month's drill will help you notice and remember the small things.

It's the small things that count when it comes to happiness, too.

Dinner is one of the things we don't really think that much about. Unless you're very poor and are only able to eat one meal a day.

But by putting your focus on this meal, you will learn to appreciate one more daily event. And you'll find out how everything can become a story if you let it.

While it's often (in my experience) difficult to involve all five senses when describing something, dinner makes it easy.

You have:

Sight
Sound
Smell
Taste
Touch

When you first sit down to write for five minutes, go for the obvious.

What did your dinner look like? What colors were involved? Did you feel like putting your fork or spoon into it and eating, or did you have to force yourself to eat it?

What sounds did you hear? Somebody chewing? A dog nearby smacking its lips, hoping to lick the plates?

What did your dinner smell like?

What did it taste like? Describe the different nuances and textures of the ingredients.

What did it feel like in your mouth? Or in your hand? Was it warm or cold?

After a while, when you're tired of describing how yesterday's cold pizza was, feel free to let your imagination take over.

Become the food.

Or become your dog waiting for you to finish and leave him something.

Or imagine that you had been starving for months

when a wealthy man invited you inside and shared his food with you.

Or watch the broccoli come to life and try to escape from your fork.

Or become an alien visiting earth for the first time and describe your spaghetti meal through their eyes.

It's all up to you, but have fun with it.

June's Drill
1. What did you have for dinner last night?
2. Describe it.

July

Your July drill is:

Pick four persons or characters and become them.

This is so much fun. I love this drill. I've published a couple of them on my BrittMalka.com blog.

Back then I didn't time myself, th0ugh, so I have no idea how long it took me to write. Probably somewhere between five and ten minutes.

It all starts with you picking four persons or characters.

They can be living persons, dead persons, or fictional characters.

The more different from you, the better.

I recommend that you choose four persons who all have a significant character trait or two.

It could be strength, confidence, faith, generosity, humor, jealousy, weakness, etc.

Here's a list of 638 primary personality traits: http://ideonomy.mit.edu/essays/traits.html

Then, you become one of those characters, a new one each week, and you write in first-person point of view as if you were that person.

Pretend you're that person, and you write a journal.

What has happened to this person? Remember, the

small daily things can be interesting.

What is that person planning to do? Are they worried about the result of their actions?

Did they just enjoy a delicious meal? What does the world look like seen through their eyes and sensed through their senses? What opinions do they hold? Why are they doing what they do?

Use all five senses if possible. The more you train yourself to do this, the easier it will be for you to include them. Here they are:

Sight
Sound
Smell
Taste
Touch

This exercise can have some interesting side-effects.

When I wrote as a villain in one of my fairy tale retellings, I learned what motived her, and it gave me sympathy for her.

This drill can also help you find your voice because it's all fun and play, nothing important here. If your chosen person is strong, daring, and confident, it will come through in your writing. And you will sound more strong, daring, and confident in your own writing after a while.

July's Drill
1. Pick four persons or characters.

2. Become them, one each week, and write like them.

August

Your August drill is:

Pick two nouns at random.

Many years ago, a writing friend and I created a script that would pick two random nouns from the base we had served it.

We had set a timer to stop after seven minutes. After the timer reached zero, we could no longer write or change the text. We could only download it.

We had lots of fun with this for months.

You can recreate the exercise thanks to a free service online and a stop watch.

Here's what you should do this month:

Search for "random noun" or use this service:

http://www.desiquintans.com/noungenerator?count=2

Bookmark the link so you have easy access to it. (I'm not in any way associated with the service, but it's easy to use and it works.)

Write for five minutes and use the two nouns as fast as possible.

This works best if you use the two nouns you get the first time each day. Don't keep trying until you find nouns you think are easier to use.

Challenge your imagination.

And if possible, include all five senses in your writing.

Sight

Sound

Smell

Taste

Touch

Have fun with this one.

August's Drill

1. Pick two nouns at random.

2. Use them in your writing.

September

Your September drill is:

Become Venus.

Okay, I have a weakness for the Renaissance era.

Ever since I, as a child, spent every summer vacation in Italy and fell in love with a statue called "La Primavera" (the spring), I've loved it.

Living in France among Renaissance castles only enforced this weakness.

So when I thought of a character from a painting, The Birth of Venus by Botticelli was the first that came to mind.

Search for it. You probably already know it, but find a picture of the painting and save it near you to use this month.

Study the painting, imagine you're the newborn Venus, and write her daily journal.

Write for five minutes as if you're Venus. It doesn't matter whether you're a man or a woman in real life. It doesn't matter if you're religious or not.

For five minutes you become a Roman goddess. (We're just playing, remember?)

A lot of successful stories and Hollywood movies rely

on a concept that is called a "fish out of water."

It means that a character suddenly finds himself in a new world.

For example, you'll see this in *Back to the Future*, where Marty McFly goes back in time.

You'll see it in *Trading Places* with Eddie Murphy, where he's a beggar, lying about being injured, and then is moved to a rich man's villa to serve as a CEO for a successful company.

That kind of story is successful in emails as well.

Could you share a "me as Venus" with your subscribers? Perhaps. It depends on your relationship with them.

At any rate, have fun with this one, and use all five senses if possible.

Sight
Sound
Smell
Taste
Touch

What does the air smell like? What is the temperature like? (Touch) What sounds surround you? What do you see? What do you taste?

You can start with one sense per day, if you prefer, and then reach all five senses within six days of writing.

Sure, you'll get bored at some point. That's fine. That's just an invitation to your imagination to run wild.

Perhaps Venus wasn't born on Earth?

Perhaps she's not the goddess of love, but something completely different?

Perhaps she's not even a woman?

You decide, and you'll know when it's time to go crazy in your writing.

September's Drill

1. Find and save a picture of "The Birth of Venus" by Botticelli.

2. Become Venus, and write your journal for five minutes.

October

Your October drill is:

Describe what you're doing seen from a pet's point of view.

For this month's drill, you'll have to imagine that four pets sit next to you:

A cat, a dog, a fish, and a bird.

The first week, you become a cat. And you (the cat) look up at you (the human) and describe what you (the human) are doing.

The second week, you become a dog and study and describe yourself (the human) from its point of view.

The third week, you become a fish.

The final week, you become a bird.

For the last three days, you can either go back to one or more of the pets, or come up with a fifth one of your choice.

In some way, I do this drill every day.

My dog, Nefnef, loves cats. She loves food above anything else, and cats come in second place.

When we walk to the park, we look for cats. I feel her excitement when we find a cat. I've followed along with joy as she "tamed" one wild cat after the other.

Back in our house, I know that when she comes running and scratches my shoulder, it means that we should go cat-spotting on the balcony.

Then again, I become her and see through her eyes, and experience through her senses and emotions.

I think you'll enjoy this exercise. Have fun with it. Use humor if you can.

I'm sure you'll act in mysterious and weird ways when you look at yourself from a pet's point of view.

If possible, use all five senses in your daily writings. They are:

Sight
Sound
Smell
Taste
Touch

October's Drill

1. Become a cat (week 1), a dog (week 2), a fish (week 3), and a bird (week 4).

2. Sit next to you (the human) and describe what you're doing.

November

Your November drill is:
Become Michelangelo's David.
I'm sure you know Michelangelo's marble statue of David, but how well do you know it?
Take a closer look.
I just searched and found an interesting article about something Michelangelo observed two centuries before it became knowledge for doctors. You can read it here:
https://www.indystar.com/story/entertainment/arts/2020/0 1/15/michelangelo-david-reveals-medical-mystery-500-years-later/4431309002/
For this month's drill, find a picture of the statue, and imagine how it would be to be David.
Would you be cold, white, and made out of stone?
Would you be scared? Or excited about the upcoming fight with Goliath?
How do you feel?
And to use all five senses in your writing, think about:

Sight - what do you, David, see? Now? Then?
Sound - what do you hear? Now? Then?
Smell - what scents drift into your nostrils?

Taste - what did your last meal taste like? Or the one you'll get as a victor?

Touch - what's the temperature like? Does the sun bake your (marble) skin? Do the floodlights burn the top of your head?

Become David, the man, the king, back then, the statue then or now, or even in the future.

Then write his journal for five minutes every day.

November's Drill
1. Find a picture of Michelangelo's David.
2. Become him, and journal as him.

December

Your December drill is:

Visit Earth as an alien.

There are plenty of holidays in December.

Usually, there are Hanukkah, Christmas, and sometimes other holidays too.

If you were an alien, visiting Earth for the first time, how would you experience those holidays?

You don't have to cover them all. Cover the holiday you celebrate yourself.

Then pick one thing from that holiday to write about in your drill daily.

For Christmas, it could be a plastic Christmas tree one day. What does it smell like? What does it feel like? Prickly? Smooth? What does a tree have to do with a child being born? What's a baby anyway?

Or it could be eggnog. What does it look like? What does it taste like? What about the smell and feel? And will you, as an alien, drink it? Or try to smoke it or even wash your tentacles with it?

For Hanukkah, it could be a Hanukkah candle. What does it smell like? What does it feel like to be near it? Hot? Cold?

Or it could be the Dreidel. What on Earth is that? A tool, a toy, food?

Or even latkes. What's all that about oil? Not having enough of it and then using oil on everything for eight days?

I'm sure there are plenty of unknown things about the December holidays to explore for an alien.

Now, you'll be that alien, so write what you find for five minutes per day.

Use all five senses when possible. You can start with one per day and work your way up to all five. They are:

Sight
Sound
Smell
Taste
Touch

Have fun with this one.

December's Drill
1. Become an alien visiting Earth for the first time.
2. Describe one thing about this month's holiday per day.

What Now?

Are you cheating?

Did you do all twelve months of drills, or did you read through them, and now you're here in the last chapter?

You may be. I know I would.

Still, if that's the case, it's fine. No worries.

What month do you have?

Just flip to that month and start doing the drills. It's okay if the date says 27. Still go to that month and write for three days.

At the end of the cycle, you can go back and start from scratch. Or come up with your own drills.

Or send me an email and ask me to write a follow-up book.

After a Year of Drills

Your writing skills will have improved. You'll have built your writing muscles.

People will notice it, and many will tell you that they love your writing.

You're now able to pick everyday situations and turn them into great stories to use for fiction books, emails, sales pages, blog posts, and even letters to friends and family.

You'll feel freer to use your imagination.

You'll be better at seeing a situation or a person from several different angles.

If you're using your stories to sell, you'll sell more.

Your writing will be more entertaining, and that's always appreciated by readers.

What's more, you'll have fun with writing.

You'll enjoy writing, because writing is fun. Writing should be fun.

Have fun.

Examples

Honestly, I wasn't sure if I should give you examples or not.

At first, I decided not to, because I want your imagination to be in charge. Not what you've seen others do.

But then I thought that maybe one of the drills was unclear to you. And I would hate it if you weren't able to do a full month's drills, just because I hadn't explained it well enough.

So here are example drills.

They are unedited, because drills are drills. They are private exercises. They are rough.

And you don't need to read them.

Use them only if you lack inspiration or aren't quite sure about a specific drill.

So here we go.

January
What is the weather like?

Sooner or later the sun will warm me up. I know that.

And I feel lucky that statistics say we'll have six hours of sun, on average. Still, it's freezing. I saw a flower, yesterday. Pretty, red, and exotic. But the cool air dampened whatever scent it might have had if it had flowered on a more appropriate time. It made me feel excited, though. Gave me hope. In a few months I will long for a cool breeze, but right now I appreciate every moment when the sun heats up my skin. Birds chirp outside my window now. One neighbor has started his stereo rack, probably just as nostalgic as I am, longing for the hot summer nights when he and his friends are dancing outside, listening to live music. I take a sip of my hot water with lemon juice. Even in the bitterness there is sweetness and a fruity taste. How can they still produce fresh lemons at this time of year? It's beyond me, but I appreciate the taste and the feeling as the water warms me up from the inside. The sky looks blue and clear with no rain in

February
Wash your hands

I turn on the faucet and cold water streams out. I adjust the handle to give me, hopefully, a little bit of hot water, if there's still some left in the heater.

There is, and now I burn my right hand slightly. The pain makes me adjust the handle again. Finally the temperature is a perfect little warmer than lukewarm. I wet my hands and I turn off the water again.

I put my left hand under the tip of the soap dispenser that contains purple fluid soap that smells of synthetic lavender. With my right hand I press the button and cold soap streams out into my left hand. It feels smooth and pleasant, and it's already reached a more pleasant temperature.

I put my two hands together and cover them with soap. The palm of my hands first, then the upper sides, then between my fingers. Faster and faster they move like dancers in the rain, white foam forming between my fingers as I rub my thumbs together, enjoying the smooth feeling of the soap.

(Britt's comment: No sound and no taste included in the text.)

March
Drink water

I've already had my usual hot water with lemon this morning. Now, at 10 O'clock, I'm waiting for my second cup of tea, and since I'm still thirsty, I sip water. Yesterday evening, I took a bottle of cold water from the refrigerator and added sparkles thanks to our Sodastream machine. I poured the last of that bottle into my glass, and that's what I'm drinking now. The bubbles are almost nonexisting, and the water is no longer quite chilled. Still, it quenches my thirst and tastes fine. Different water can have different taste. This one tastes nice thanks to being filtered tap-water. I enjoy the feeling as it cools the inner of my mouth and down my throat when I swallow. It has no smell. When it's freshly made, it tingles when I pour the water into my glass. But now, with the few and tiny bubbles, not a sound is coming from my glass. I just see two or three lost bubbles at the bottom of the clear water.

April
Pick one event that happened the day before

Nefnef and I had reached the far end of the park. In spite of the cold temperature, around 12 degrees Celcius, there were plenty of people relaxing on the benches and even on the grass, enjoying the sun. I raised my head and felt the sun's warmth on my skin. I inhaled and picked up a faint scent of the sea that filled half my view.

Nefnef dragged her leash, wanting to go on.

A man closed in on us. He was wrapped in a short, brown coat, wore the mandatory facemask and a hood. I didn't recognize him.

As we passed him, he said, "It's 3 O'clock."

"Exactly," I said, knowing that it wasn't true. I didn't wear a watch, haven't done so for years, but I knew that it was more likely around a quarter to three, because Nefnef and I usually leave home at 2:30 in the afternoon.

I had spoken with the man before, but I still don't recognize his face for some strange reason. All I know is that he's Russian and knew that I walked my dog at the same time every afternoon.

It's

(Britt's comment: No taste included in the text.)

May
Find four books
Handcopy the beginning

(This is pretty straightforward, so there's no need for an example.)

June
Dinner the day before

Last night we started with a salad that contained lettuce,

cheese cubes, and tomatoes with a dressing consisting of vinegar and olive oil. It tasted nice, although I'm not that crazy about lettuce.

It looked great, though, with its green, red, and light-yellow colors. A symphony for the eyes.

I bit into the spongy light-yellow cheese bites and enjoyed the taste. Then I stabbed my fork into the green leaves on my plate, trying to stack them up instead of eating one tiny bit after the other.

After that, we had our main meal that consisted of fried turkey and fried potatoes. I shouldn't eat potatoes, but I must confess that they tasted good. So did the turkey. It was fried in sesam oil, and the smell and the taste is nutty and very delicious.

I left two bites on my plate. Nefnef clucked her tongue several times in anticipation of licking our plates when we were done.

July
Pick four persons/characters

One of my characters was Carabosse, the evil fairy godmother from *Sleeping Beauty*.

I have to find somebody to clean this room. Cob webs every where. Where is that lazy chamber maid? They probably think that I was too old and weak to see what a slobby job they did.

But I am not weak. My powers grow day for day, and soon the princess will turn 16. Soon she'll fall for the curse, and I am free. Free to grow my powers for the next hundred years.

I'd sworn to revenge the humility bestowed upon me by fairy Jane. People think I'm dead, now, because nothing bad has happened to Jane. Yet. They had no idea how patient I can be. I will get my revenge in the end, and I don't mind waiting.

It feels good to have something to live for.

As I glance through the tower window, my pet dragon flies by. He is no bigger than a cat, but still mighty powerful. The woods around the building withered and died under his tiny flames. The earth is scorched and no new life takes form here.

August
Find two random nouns.
My two nouns were: basket - reading

When Lisa came back from school that day, she found her mother sitting on the floor in her room next to the waste basked, reading crumbled pieces of paper.

"Mom?"

Her mother looked up. She looked like a toad trying to swallow a hornet without getting stung.

"Mom, are you all right?" She threw her bag on the floor and rushed towards her mother. "Do you want a glass of water or something?"

In all the movies she'd seen where people had been in shock, water had always been the best remedy.

Her mother shook her head. Apparently, they hadn't been watching the same movies.

"These..." Her mother lifted her palms, filled with crumbled balls of paper. "Did you write them?"

Lisa couldn't be sure based on a quick glance, but who else would write something and throw it in the basket in her room? She nodded. "I must have. Why?"

"Why?" Her mother yelled now. "Are you freaking crazy?"

(Britt's comment: No smell, touch, or taste in this one.)

September
Become Venus

Image: Wikimedia.org

It's all blurry.

I have no recollection of where I came from. I know who I am. I'm Venus.

My feet are dry thanks to the sea shell I'm standing on. Otherwise the clucking water beneath it would have covered my feet, and perhaps chilled my legs up to my knees.

It's cold, and Zephyr's blowing icy air on me doesn't make things better. Luckily, a kind woman is about to cover me with a blanket that looks both soft and warm.

The air smells of sweet flowers and salty sea. My stomach growls. I can't wait to have my first meal. How will it taste? Like flowers and wind? Like fish and sea?

What awaits me on the shores of this country? Will I be naked like Zephyr or clad in a loose

October

Become a cat, a dog, a fish, and a bird sit next to you

For this drill, I'm my dog, Nefnef.

How come Mom doesn't see me? I stare at her. She has to see me. That chicken smells so good. I love chicken. It tastes so good, like nothing else I know.

Mom has given me a blanket to sit on. It's good. The floor is cold at this time of the year. I love sitting on the balcony, but Mom says it's too cold. So I sit on my blanket, and it feels good. It's soft and warm and it smells of me and a little bit of Frostie.

Frostie is a cat. I love him, and I love to play with him,

but I don't want him to sit on my blanket. It's my blanket, says Mom.

Mom looks at a big screen with moving colors while she's eating chicken. She's eating vegetables, too. I don't like vegetables. I like smelling them when Mom and Dad get a box of them. They smell of animals I have never seen. A little bit like that rat Mom and I saw outside. And like the hedgehog.

I want to take them with me in to play, but Mom said no. I love all animals. Especially cats. But it's my blanket. Mom says so. She even tells Frostie to move away from it when he tries to steal it.

(Britt's comment: no sound in this one.)

November
Become Michelangelo's David

Image: Wikimedia.org

This is not how I visualized it would go. I'm standing here in a cold room, completely naked except for my sling. And I'm waiting for Goliath who should have been here thousands of years ago. And I'm still waiting.

The room smells dusty. Not at all like the green fields I grew up on, where grass would spread their juicy scents in the air whenever a sheep took a nip. Baah'ing all the time, they were, but I prefer that sound any time over the sound of whispering Japanese men and women armed with cameras. Or yelling kids, whirling around the fragile pedestal I'm standing on. With bare feet. Go ahead and do that, just for a few minutes. Stand on a cold, hard block of marble, cut like broken, hard earth, just for a few minutes. I would love to see you do that without whining for a warm foot bath.

Speaking of bath. A shower would be nice. Sure, somebody comes once in a while and dust my skin, but I still remember the silent rain falling on my shoulders in the fields outside of Jerusalem. The golden city.

How I long to go back, maybe grab a falafel sandwich in a pita bread and taste the

(Britt's comment: I didn't have time to finish writing about taste.)

December
You are an alien from outer space, visiting Earth, and describe one thing about this month's holiday each day

It's the third time I watch these people through the

window. It's dark outside where I am, but light, just like the day, where the people are locked in. They seem to stare out of me, but I know they don't see me, because I've made myself invisible to them.

I can't figure out what they are doing. It doesn't seem logical at all.

They have this…thing. I don't know what it is. It smells through the window as if it was made out of metal. The red golden one we have so much of on our planet. If we don't clean and polish it, it turns green. But this thing is red and smells of that red-green metal. It has a round foot, just one foot, not four like we have. It has one leg, not four like us, and then it has two arms, not four like we have.

On those arms are small cups. Nine cups.

One of the persons, a tall one with hair all over his face, holds a burning stick in his hands and makes sounds. I don't understand what he's saying. I was told that people here spoke English, and I had learned that language, but this is nothing like it.

Yesterday he put two burning sticks in three of the cups. The first day it was only two, but today there are four. It's weird. Why have nine cups if they only put burning sticks in some of them?

And what are they for? Food?

(Britt's comment: No taste in this one.)

Author Bio

Britt Malka quit her day-job in 1995 to become a full-time writer.

She has lived in four different countries, Denmark, Germany, France, and since 2011, in Israel.

She loves to read and write books to help others gain freedom and live the life they desire.

When she's not writing, she's playing an old version of World of Warcraft with her husband, walking her dog, Nefnef, splitting up pet fights between Nefnef and the cat, Frostie, or learning Hebrew.

You can sign up to get notified about new books if you visit her homepage at https://BrittMalka.com.

Supersize Your Story-Telling Skills

Scan me

Also by Britt Malka

Nonfiction

Curation Templates: Your 5 Shortcuts to Evergreen Blog Posts
The Zefram Blogging System: Your Guide to Warp Speed Blogging and a Never-Ending Galaxy of Ideas
How to Stop Procrastinating: Beat Procrastination Now... Not Tomorrow
How to Explain Things: A Writer's Guide
10-Minute Emails: Writing Better Emails in Shorter Time (Email Marketing Basics)

Fiction

A Model for Murder
Amber Alert

Mystery Book Club
And Hope to Dye